From Broken to Blessed

Breaking Free from Addiction and Finding Purpose

By

Christina Jackson

ISBN

978-1-966355-11-3

Table of Contents

Prologue

"He heals the brokenhearted and binds up their wounds."

~Psalm 147:3

I never imagined my life would turn out this way. If you had told me years ago that I would be here sober, standing in faith, and using my voice to inspire others. I would have laughed in disbelief. My life was chaos, a never-ending cycle of addiction, pain, and survival. I had lost nearly everything: my children, my dignity, my health, and, at times, even my will to live. But God had other plans.

For almost two decades, I was trapped in a life that wasn't my own. Addiction wrapped its chains around me, dragging me into a darkness so deep that I thought I would never escape. I was a mother who couldn't mother, a daughter who lost both parents too soon, a woman who had been beaten down by life, by men, by the choices I made and the ones that were made for me. I prostituted to survive. I went to jail. I lived in places no human should ever have to live. I held my breath every time I stuck a needle in my arm, wondering if this time would be my last.

Even in my darkest moments, God never left me. He sent people to pray for me when I couldn't pray for myself. He whispered warnings when danger was near. He gave me a chance after chance, waiting for me to surrender, to trust, to finally break free.

This book isn't just my story. It is a testimony that no one is too lost to be found, no one is too broken to be restored, and no life is too far gone for redemption. It's proof that even when we feel unworthy, unloved, and unseen, God is still working behind the scenes, shaping our pain into purpose.

If you are struggling, if you feel hopeless, if you've made mistakes, or if you think you can never recover from them, I want you to know there is hope. There is a way out. There is a new life waiting for you on the other side of surrender.

This is my story. Not just of addiction but of survival. Not just of loss but of restoration. Not just of pain but of grace.

Chapter 1

Who I Am Today?

"For I know the plans I have for you,"
declares the Lord, "plans to prosper you
and not to harm you, plans to give you
hope and a future."
~Jeremiah 29:11

If someone had told me years ago that I would one day stand before others as a minister, a leader, and a testimony of God's grace, I would have thought they were crazy. Me? A minister? A woman with my past? The woman who had lost herself to addiction, who had been in and out of jail, who had lost her children to the system? There was no way. I was too far gone. At least, that's what I believed for a long time. However, God had a plan even when I couldn't see it.

Today, I am no longer the woman the streets tried to destroy. I am no longer bound by addiction, shame, or the pain of my past. I am redeemed. I am a mother, a minister, and the founder of a non-profit organization dedicated to helping people who are struggling the way I once was.

But getting here was a journey. And this is where it begins.

The Woman I Am Today

When I look in the mirror now, I see someone I never thought I would become. I see strength. I see a purpose. I see grace.

I am a woman who has walked through fire and came out on the other side, not burned but refined. Every scar tells a story. Every tear I shed was not wasted. God took the most broken parts of my life and used them to build something beautiful.

I am a minister. Not because I am perfect but because I am proof of God's mercy. I know what it feels like to be lost, and now I help others find their way. I don't just preach about redemption.

I am a mother. After years of addiction and years of losing custody of my children, I am now raising two of them, one of whom I had to fight for custody of. In 2006, I had my second child, but by that time, addiction had already taken a deep hold on my life. I wanted to be the mother my children deserved, but the battle with drugs made it nearly impossible to give them the stability and love they needed.

There was a time when I believed I would never be able to be the mother my children needed. God restores what was lost. My journey as a mother has not been easy, but every moment I get to spend with them now is a gift I don't take for granted.

I am the founder of a non-profit. My non-profit is more than an organization; it's a mission. It's a way to reach people who are where I once was. It's a way to offer hope to the hopeless, to show them that they are not forgotten. Whether it's helping someone find a rehab program, giving them food and shelter, or simply praying with them in their lowest moments, this is my calling.

My Mission: Why I Do This Work

I never want another woman, another mother, or another child to feel the way I once did: trapped, hopeless, and beyond saving.

That's why I do what I do. Because I know what it feels like.

- I know what it's like to wake up and feel like you have nothing left to live for.
- I know what it's like to have your children taken away, to feel like you've failed as a mother.

- I know what it's like to cry out to God, begging for Him to take the pain away.

And I also know what it's like to be saved.

I know what it's like to wake up one day and feel a shift in your spirit. To realize that God has been there all along, waiting for you to surrender. To finally step into life, He planned for you before the world tried to break you.

That's why I get up every day and do this work.

That's why I talk to people who are still in addiction, who are still on the streets, who are still suffering. Because I know the power of transformation, and I want them to know it too.

Why I Am Writing This Book

For years, I believed my story was a tragedy. Now I know it's a testimony.

I am writing this book for the ones who are still struggling. For the ones who think their mistakes are too great, their past too messy, their future too uncertain. For the ones who feel like there's no way out.

- If you are battling addiction, this book is for you.

- If you have lost your children and feel like you'll never get them back, this book is for you.
- If you have been beaten down by life and feel like you don't deserve a second chance, this book is for you.

Because I am living proof that **God restores.**

This is not just my story but a message of hope. It's a declaration that no one is too lost to be found, that no mistake is too big for God to forgive, and that no pain is too deep for Him to heal.

I am writing this book because someone out there needs to read it.

Someone needs to know that their story isn't over. That God is still writing their chapters. That there is still time to turn things around.

I hope that as you read this, you will see that if God could save me, He can save you, too.

I hope you will find the courage to believe in a new beginning.

I hope you will find the strength to keep going.

Because your story is far from over.

Chapter 2

My Childhood and Early Life

"Train up a child in the way he should go; even when he is old, he will not depart from it."
~Proverbs 22:6

Before the struggles, before the addiction, before the pain, there was a little girl full of dreams, hope, and innocence. That little girl was me.

When I look back at my childhood, I see two versions of it. One version is filled with love, laughter, and the warmth of my father's presence. The other version is clouded by fear, confusion, and the reality of my mother's schizophrenia. The contrast between those two worlds shaped me in ways I wouldn't fully understand until later in life.

I didn't know then how much my childhood would impact the choices I would make as an adult. I didn't realize that some of the lessons I learned about love, survival, and pain would follow me for years. Now, as I reflect, I can see how every moment, both good and bad, played a part in shaping the person I became.

My Upbringing and Family Background

I was born into a home where love and struggle coexisted. My father was my world, my protector, my provider, my everything. He worked tirelessly Monday through Friday, making sure we had what we needed. No matter how hard things got, he never let me feel the weight of the world on my shoulders. On weekends, that changed. My father was a functioning alcoholic.

Throughout the week, he was the man I admired most. When Friday night came, the alcohol took over. He would come home drunk, his steps unsteady, his words slurred. It was a different version of him, one that made me anxious, one that reminded me that even the strongest people have their weaknesses. Even then, I never doubted his love for me. I was a daddy's girl. If you saw him, you saw me.

My mother's presence in my life was much different. She suffered from schizophrenia, and as a child, I didn't understand what that meant. I only knew that some days she seemed fine, and other days, it was like she was in an entirely different world.

Mental illness is terrifying when you're a child. I watched my mother's moods shift unpredictably and saw her struggle with things that didn't make sense to me. At times, I was afraid, afraid of what was happening to her, afraid of what I couldn't understand. But despite her illness, she did the best she could. She loved me in her own way, even if our relationship was distant.

Key Childhood Memories

Some of my childhood memories are filled with warmth and security. I remember him making time for me no matter how tired he was from work, taking me places, and making me feel important.

But then there were the moments that forced me to grow up too soon.

I remember the weekends when my father would come home drunk, stumbling through the door, his voice louder than usual. I would watch him, but I was unsure of what version of him I would get. I never felt unsafe, but I felt the shift, the change in his energy. I knew that for the next two days, things wouldn't be the same.

I remember watching my mother struggle with her illness, seeing her act in ways that scared me and made me question what was happening inside her mind. Some days, she would be okay. Other days, she wasn't. And on those days, I felt helpless.

I remember feeling alone, realizing that beyond the walls of our home, we didn't have the kind of family I saw other kids talk about.

My Relationship with My Parents and Early Experiences That Shaped Me

My father was my rock. I never doubted his love. He worked hard, he provided, and no matter what, I always knew he was there for me. Even when he drank on the weekends, I still saw him as the man who held our world together. He was my protector, my hero, the person I felt safest with.

My relationship with my mother was more complicated. It wasn't that she didn't love me, but there was always a distance between us, a gap that I didn't know how to bridge. I wanted to feel close to her, but her illness stood in the way.

Growing up in my home shaped the way I viewed love, survival, and struggle. It taught me that love can exist even in brokenness, that people can be strong in one way and weak in another, and that sometimes, you have to learn how to stand on your own.

I didn't know then what the future held. I didn't know that loss was waiting for me just around the corner.

But I do know this: my childhood, with all its beauty and all its pain, was the beginning of a story that was only just unfolding.

Chapter 3

The Beginning of Struggles

"The Lord is close to the brokenhearted and saves those who are crushed in spirit."
~Psalm 34:18

At 15 years old, my world shattered.

My mother died suddenly. One day, she was there. And the next, she wasn't.

I had spent my entire childhood watching her struggle, knowing that something wasn't right, knowing that there was a distance between us that I didn't know how to fix. When she was gone, I realized something heartbreaking: I would never have another chance to fix it.

Losing My Mother and How It Affected Me

There is a difference between losing someone slowly and losing someone suddenly. One lets you prepare, and the other leaves you in shock. I never got the chance to say goodbye to my mother. I never got to have those last words, that final moment of closure. She was just gone.

I had always thought that, despite her struggles, she would be around forever. That one day, we would have a better relationship, and we would find a way to bridge the distance between us. But life didn't give us that chance.

When my mother passed, I felt so many emotions at once: grief, guilt, confusion, and even anger. I didn't know how to process it.

I felt guilty for not being closer to her while she was alive. I felt confused about what my life would look like without her. And I was angry that she left, angry that I didn't understand her when she was here, angry that I never got the chance to fix things.

For days after her death, I barely spoke. Everything around me felt unreal as if I was walking through a dream I couldn't wake up from. I would hear people talking and feel their hands on my shoulder as they whispered their condolences, but it was like they were speaking a different language. Nothing felt real.

I held all my emotions inside because I didn't know what else to do with them. I didn't know how to grieve.

Even as my life spiraled, something in me wanted to hold onto a piece of my future. I made the decision to take my GED exam (2003). It felt like the last thing I could control in a life that was already slipping away from me.

And then, before I could even begin to heal, life delivered another blow.

My Father's Hospitalization and Passing

My father was never the same after my mother died.

Grief changes people. It takes everything strong in them and weakens them, pulling them into a darkness they don't know how to escape from. And that's exactly what happened to my father.

I had always known him to be a strong man, a provider, someone who made sure we were okay no matter what. After my mother passed, I watched that strength fade away. He stopped taking care of himself and stopped trying to hold it all together.

And he drank even more.

He had always been a functioning alcoholic, drinking on the weekends but pulling himself together for the workweek. After my mother was gone, the drinking became something else. It wasn't just on the weekends anymore. It wasn't just a habit.

I saw the man who had been my rock slowly crumble before my eyes.

Then, one day, he was gone too.

When I was 16 years old, my father passed away.

The Moment My World Fell Apart

Losing my father felt different from losing my mother.

With my mother, there was sadness, regret, and confusion. Whereas, with my father, there was fear.

I had always been a daddy's girl. If you saw him, you saw me. He was my safe place, my protector, my everything. And now, he was gone.

I remember feeling completely untethered like I was floating in space with nothing to hold onto. I had lost both of my parents within a year.

And suddenly, I was alone.

There was no safety net. No extended family to step in and take me in. No one told me what was going to happen next.

The reality of my situation hit me hard. I wasn't just grieving; and I was trying to survive.

At that moment, I had two choices: fight or escape.

And I didn't know how to fight.

The Breaking Point: My First Encounter with Drugs

Grief and loneliness are a dangerous combination. When you have nothing left, you will do anything to stop feeling empty. And that's exactly what happened to me.

I wasn't trying to ruin my life. I wasn't trying to become an addict.

I just wanted the pain to stop.

On the day of my mother's funeral, someone handed me meth, and in that moment of unbearable grief, I took it without hesitation. I didn't think about the consequences. I didn't care. I just wanted everything to go numb.

For the first time since losing her, I felt a sense of relief. The suffocating weight in my chest lightened. The world, which had been spinning out of control, seemed to pause. My thoughts slowed, the grief dulled, and for a brief moment, I felt okay.

And that was all it took.

I told myself it was just for that night, just something to get me through the worst of it. But addiction doesn't work like that.

Addiction doesn't knock on your door and introduce itself; it sneaks in quietly, disguised as relief.

And once it has you, it doesn't let go.

That one hit was the beginning of something that would take years to escape.

The Shift from Pain to Survival

After that first time, I convinced myself that it was temporary. That I wouldn't let it take over my life. The thing about drugs is that they don't just numb the pain; they make you crave more.

The next time I was overwhelmed, the next time I felt lost, the next time I didn't know what to do, I reached for it again.

And then again.

At first, I thought I was in control. In reality, I had already lost control.

By the time my father passed, I wasn't just using meth anymore.

His death only pushed me further into the depths of addiction. The grief, the loneliness, the overwhelming reality of being without both of my parents. The drugs weren't just an escape anymore. They were a necessity.

After my parents passed, I wasn't completely alone, and I had my sister. She took care of me and gave me a place to stay. I wasn't homeless, but that didn't mean I wasn't lost. Grief still consumed me, and addiction had already taken hold, pulling me further away from the life I once knew.

I grew up with siblings, but there was always a gap between us. My older siblings were much older than me, and because of that, we didn't play together the way some brothers and sisters do. I also had a half-brother who was raised by my grandmother, so our lives followed different paths. Despite this, family was still a part of my life in different ways.

Beyond family, I had friends in the neighborhood. There were kids I played with, people who were part of my everyday world.

Even in the midst of my struggles, those friendships were there, giving me moments of normalcy in a life that often felt anything but normal.

The Downward Spiral Begins

When I was 16 years old, I had already lost everything.

My childhood was gone. My parents were gone. And now, I was disappearing, too.

Drugs gave me a way to forget the pain. What I didn't realize at the time was that they were also taking away pieces of me, little by little.

I started hanging around the wrong people, people who didn't ask questions, who didn't care about what I had been through.

I stopped thinking about the future.

Because how do you think about the future when you don't even know how to survive the present?

At 16 years old, I had gone from being a daughter to being an orphan.

And the only thing I knew how to do was survive.

The Beginning of My Struggles

When people talk about addiction, they don't talk about how easy it is to fall into it. They don't talk about the way it starts as a whisper in the back of your mind, just this once, just to make it through today, until it becomes a scream you can't silence.

At 16 years old, I had no one.

No home.

No parents.

No direction.

And so, I turned to the only thing that made the pain go away.

I didn't know it at the time, but this was the moment my life changed forever.

This was the beginning of my struggles.

And at the time, I had no idea just how dark things were about to get.

Chapter 4

The Deepening of Addiction

"For what I want to do, I do not do, but what I hate, I do."
~Romans 7:15

There is a moment when addiction stops being a habit and becomes your whole identity. At first, I thought I was just using it to escape my pain, but before I knew it, drugs became my master. My life revolved around them and finding them, using them, recovering just enough to go out and find more. Everything else faded into the background.

I told myself that I was still in control. That I could stop whenever I wanted. That I was still a mother, still a woman with responsibilities. Those were lies I fed myself to avoid facing the truth. And the truth was that I had lost control.

The Challenges of Being a Young Mother Battling Addiction

Motherhood is supposed to be sacred. It is supposed to be the one thing that forces you to pull yourself together to push through any hardship because another life is depending on you. That's what I told myself I would do.

But addiction is stronger than logic. Stronger than love. Stronger than any promise you make to yourself in the moments of clarity when you think, "This is it. I'm done."

I wanted to be a good mother. I wanted to be the kind of mother my own had been: loving, strong, always present. But addiction stole that from me. I would wake up and promise myself that today would be different, that I wouldn't use, that I would stay clean and take care of my child. By midday, the withdrawal would start creeping in, the shakes, the nausea, the unbearable feeling of my skin crawling. My body would scream for a fix, and suddenly, nothing else mattered.

I hated myself for it. I hated that I would leave my baby with family members or friends just so I could go get high. I hated that when I held my child; all I could think about was when I would get my next hit. The guilt consumed me, but instead of getting better, I used even more to make that guilt go away.

I told myself I wasn't a bad mother. I convinced myself that as long as my baby was fed and had a roof over their head, I was doing okay. However, deep down, I knew that wasn't true. Deep down, I knew that my child deserved better than a mother who was slowly destroying herself.

By 2005, I had my own place, but it didn't bring the independence or peace I thought it would. Instead, it became a space where my addiction deepened, a place where I was alone with my demons.

The Introduction to Harder Substances: Cocaine and Heroin

Meth had been my escape, but it didn't take long for me to chase something stronger. When I met my second child's father, he introduced me to cocaine and heroin.

At first, I was hesitant. I had seen what heroin had done to others. I had seen people turn into hollow versions of themselves, their lives consumed by the needle. My addiction already taken root, and the promise of something even stronger, something that could take away every ounce of pain I was feeling, was too tempting to resist.

The first time I used heroin, I felt like I had finally found peace. Every worry, every burden, every ounce of pain I carried disappeared. I felt weightless like nothing in the world could touch me. What I didn't realize then was that heroin doesn't set you free.

The high didn't last long, and when it faded, the withdrawal hit like a train. My body ached, my stomach turned, and my skin felt like it was on fire. I remember lying in bed, drenched in sweat, shaking uncontrollably, feeling like I was dying. My child's father told me there was only one way to make it stop: more heroin.

And that's how it happens. That's how heroin gets its claws into you.

At first, you do it because you want to. Then, you do it because you have to.

For a long time, I told myself that I would never use needles and that I would never become "one of those addicts." I stuck to snorting, convincing myself that I still had some control. But after losing my child, everything changed.

The pain of that loss was unbearable, and at that moment, I didn't care about the promises I had made to myself. I didn't care about boundaries, and I swore I would never cross them. I just wanted to numb the emptiness inside me.

That's when I started shooting up.

It didn't take long before I was fully dependent. I couldn't go a single day without it. My body needed it just to function, just to feel normal. And once you reach that point, you will do anything to make sure you never have to go through withdrawal again.

The Cycle of Dependency and Its Impact on My Life and Relationships

As my addiction deepened, my relationships suffered. My child's father and I weren't in love; we were two addicts clinging to each other, enabling each other, destroying each other. We spent our days chasing the next high, living from place to place, doing whatever we had to do to survive.

Addiction is selfish. It makes you push away the people who love you the most. It convinces you that they are the problem, that they don't understand, that they are the ones trying to control you.

I became a ghost in my own life. I stopped showing up for family events. I stopped answering calls. I disappeared for days at a time. The only people I surrounded myself with were other addicts because they didn't judge me. They didn't tell me to get help. They were drowning just like I was.

I knew I was spiraling. I knew I was on a path that only led to two places: prison or death. However, knowing it and stopping it were two very different things.

Losing Custody of My Children and Involvement with CPS

The moment CPS knocked on my door, I knew my time had run out.

I was staying at my child's father's mother's house when he woke me up in a panic. My child was crying, and when I looked down, I saw that his leg was swollen and bent in a way that didn't look right.

We rushed to the hospital, my heart pounding. I didn't know what had happened. I didn't know how my baby had been hurt. However, none of that mattered because when the doctors saw the injury, they called Child Protective Services.

A few days later, there was a knock at my door. I opened it to find CPS standing there, telling me that they were taking my child.

I tried to fight. I tried to plead with them. But deep down, I knew.

I knew that I wasn't a fit mother.

I knew that my child deserved better than me.

I knew that I had failed.

I broke down in the CPS office, watching them take my baby away. I was devastated, but I now understand that God knew what was best. My child was placed with my aunt, a woman who would love and care for them in a way that I wasn't capable of doing at the time.

Losing my child pushed me over the edge. I had always told myself that I would never use needles, that I wasn't 'that kind' of addict. That promise shattered after CPS took my baby. By 2006, I was injecting heroin just to get through the day.

Instead of getting clean, I used even more. The pain was unbearable, and I didn't know how to live with it. Over time, I had more children, but the pattern remained the same. Every time I thought I could get clean, I fell right back into it.

One by one, my children were taken from me and placed with family members who could give them what I couldn't.

I should have fought harder. I should have done more. But at the time, I didn't know how.

Looking back now, I see the destruction I left in my wake. I see the children who needed me, the family who loved me, the opportunities I threw away. At the time, all I could see was the next high.

This was the reality of addiction. It didn't just steal my life; it stole my ability to love, to care, and to be the person I was meant to be.

I was a mother in name only. And that truth still haunts me.

Chapter 5

Hitting Rock Bottom

"The sacrifices of God are a broken spirit; a broken and contrite heart, O God, you will not despise."
~Psalm 51:17

Addiction takes everything from you. It starts with your peace, then your dignity, then your relationships. And before you even realize what's happening, it has taken your entire life.

By the time I hit rock bottom, I had lost almost everything that mattered to me. I had lost my children. I had lost myself. And soon, I would experience another devastating loss, one that would change me forever.

Addiction doesn't just take your freedom; it takes your dignity, your self-worth, and your soul. By the time I hit rock bottom, I had lost everything. I had lost my children, my body was worn from drug use, my life was consumed by survival, and my spirit felt completely broken.

But the worst part wasn't just what I had lost; and it was that I no longer cared if I lived or died.

At this point, I wasn't just using drugs; and I was fully enslaved to them. And in that darkness, I found myself trapped in situations I once thought I'd never be in.

I thought heroin was the worst it could get. Then, someone told me that crack could help me come down from the sickness of heroin withdrawal. The moment I smoked it, I was hooked. By 2007, crack had me in a chokehold, and I felt even more out of control than before

The Descent into Prostitution and Legal Troubles

Prostitution wasn't a choice.

By the time my addiction had me in a chokehold, I had burned through every other means of getting money. My family had done all they could, and at some point, even the people who once helped me had to walk away. The drugs came first, and I would do whatever it took to get them.

At first, I told myself it wasn't "real" prostitution. I convinced myself I was just hustling, just getting what I needed to get by. But addiction doesn't give you the luxury of self-deception for long. Before I knew it, I was selling myself just to make it through the day.

I remember nights spent in absolute fear, knowing I was putting myself in danger but feeling powerless to stop. Men who didn't care if I lived or died. Places that felt like death traps. Nights where I wasn't sure if I would make it out alive.

It was terrifying. It was degrading. But at the time, it felt like my only option.

And then there were the arrests.

Jail became a revolving door. Possession charges. Petty theft. Loitering. Every time I got locked up, I told myself, *maybe this is my wake-up call.* The moment I got out, the streets called me right back.

At one point, I even contracted Hepatitis C, another consequence of the lifestyle I was living. My body was deteriorating, my mind was numb, and my soul felt completely lost.

The Moment I Realized I Needed Change

People talk about "hitting rock bottom" as if it's one single event. But for me, rock bottom happened over and over again.

There were so many moments when I thought, *this is it. This is my lowest point.*

- The nights I was so sick from heroin withdrawal that I thought I was going to die.
- The time I was raped at gunpoint and thought my life would end right there.
- The moment I realized I was pregnant again, my body was too damaged to carry the baby safely.
- That night, I had a hit out on me for robbing a drug dealer, and I had to run for my life.

Each moment should have been enough to make me stop. But the drugs wouldn't let me.

In 2017, I experienced another devastating loss. My baby was stillborn. I had already lost so much: my parents, my children, and myself, but this loss crushed me in a way I can't describe. I blamed myself, my addiction, and my choices. And instead of grieving, I used even more.

Losing My Niece and Its Impact on Me

My niece wasn't just family; but she was like a sister to me. We had always been close. Even in the depths of my addiction, she was there. She never judged me. She never turned her back on me.

And then, on January 1, 2021, she was gone.

She overdosed on fentanyl, and suddenly, the girl who had always been my little sister was just a memory.

I had already lost my parents. I had lost my children. I had lost myself.

For the first time, I truly understood what people meant when they said, "Some have to die for others to live."

That was my wake-up call.

Prayers and Seeking God's Help

I had spent years running from God.

I believed in Him. I knew He was there. But I also believed that I was too far gone, too broken, too lost to ever be saved.

For the first time in a long time, I got on my knees and prayed.

I didn't have the right words. I didn't know what to say. All I could do was cry and beg God to help me.

"God, if You're still there, if You still love me, if there is any way for me to be saved... please help me."

And at that moment, I felt something I hadn't felt in years: hope.

It wasn't immediate. It wasn't a sudden, miraculous transformation. But for the first time in a long time, I believed that maybe, just maybe, my story wasn't over.

I had prayed before, but this time was different.

I knew that if I didn't get out, I was going to die. And I wasn't ready to die anymore.

The First Step Toward Redemption

Hitting rock bottom wasn't just about losing everything. It was about realizing that I didn't want to die this way.

I didn't want my children to remember me like this.

I didn't want my life to end in a jail cell, on the streets, or overdosed in a trap house.

I wanted something different.

I wanted a second chance.

Chapter 6

The Journey to Recovery

"For I know the plans I have for you,
declares the Lord, plans to prosper you
and not to harm you, plans to give you a
future and a hope."
~ Jeremiah 29:11

For years, I had been running. Running from my pain. Running from my past. Running from God.

But in October 2020, everything changed.

I didn't know it at the time, but God had been setting the stage for my deliverance. He had been waiting for me to reach the end of myself so that I could finally turn to Him. This was my turning point. This was where my story would take a new direction.

In 2020, I experienced a medical emergency that should have killed me. My placenta abrupted, and I flatlined three times. When I woke up in the hospital, I was under investigation for my baby's death. The weight of it all was crushing. I knew I had to change, or I wouldn't make it out alive.

The Turning Point in 2020

I had been getting high all day and gambling at the same time when, out of nowhere, I hit big. I should have been happy and excited even then. But instead, I felt something shift inside me.

For years, I had been stuck in a cycle of addiction, homelessness, arrests, and loss. I had lost my children, my health, and almost my life. But now, standing there with my winnings in hand, I heard a voice in my spirit say, "This is your chance to walk away."

At that moment, I made a decision:

"I am not going to let anyone's behavior cause me to continue harming myself."

I knew if I didn't change, I was going to die of my addiction. I had ignored God's warnings for years, but this time, I couldn't ignore them any longer.

I left the toxic relationship I was in and went back to Dallas, hoping for a fresh start.

Surrendering to God's Will

For years, I had tried to fight my addiction on my own. I had moments of sobriety, but I always fell back because I was relying on my own strength.

I fell to my knees and surrendered my life to Him completely.

"God, I can't do this without You. Take this addiction away from me. If You save me, I promise I will help others the way You are helping me."

And from that moment forward, I began to see His hand in everything.

The Struggles and Victories in My Path to Sobriety

The road to recovery wasn't easy.

For almost 20 years, addiction had been my identity. I didn't know who I was without it.

There were moments when the cravings hit so hard, I thought I would break. There were nights when the pain of my past felt unbearable. This time, instead of running to drugs, I ran to God.

Instead of chasing my next high, I chased after His presence.

The withdrawals were brutal. The enemy tried everything to pull me back: temptation, triggers, old friends showing up out of nowhere. And, I was done.

I started praying every single day, asking God to remove the desire from me.

And He did.

Slowly but surely, my mind cleared, my body healed, and my spirit was restored.

The people who once saw me as a lost cause started to see a different version of me: a woman who was being transformed by the grace of God.

It wasn't an instant process. There were still struggles, still moments of doubt. For the first time in years, I believed I had a future.

And that future included getting my children back.

Regaining Custody and Rebuilding Relationships with My Children

I have been pregnant a total of 12 times, resulting in 10 deliveries. Sadly, I lost two of my children, and at the time I began my journey, I had seven living kids. After getting clean, I welcomed my last baby, bringing my total to eight living children.

For years, I had carried guilt, knowing that my addiction had cost me my children. I had watched them grow up from a distance, knowing that I had been absent in the most critical years of their lives.

But God wasn't just restoring me; and He was restoring my family.

One by one, He gave me the opportunity to rebuild my relationships with my children.

For some, it was easier than others. My youngest children were still open to having me in their lives, but for my older ones, the wounds ran deep. They had been hurt too many times before.

I knew that words wouldn't be enough; I had to show them that I was different.

So I started showing up.

I stayed clean. I prayed over them. I kept my promises.

And eventually, they saw the change in me.

It wasn't an overnight process, but by the grace of God, I was able to fight for custody of one of my children and win.

Today, I am raising two of my kids, and I am working every day to heal and rebuild my relationships with others.

A New Life in Christ

Recovery isn't just about staying sober. It's about becoming the person God created you to be.

Today, I am not just sober.

- I am a minister.
- I am the founder of a non-profit organization.
- I am a mother fighting for her children.
- I am a woman walking in God's purpose.

For years, I believed my life was over.

But now I see God was preparing me all along.

Every moment of pain, every wrong turn, every loss, it was all leading me to this moment.

A moment where I can stand before others and say, "If God can save me, He can save you too."

This is not the end of my story.

This is only the beginning.

Chapter 7

A New Purpose; Redemption and Ministry

"For I know the plans I have for you," declares the Lord, "plans to prosper you and not to harm you, plans to give you a future and a hope."
~Jeremiah 29:11

For years, I thought my story was over. I had lost my parents. I had lost my children. I had lost myself. Addiction had stolen everything from me, and for a long time, I believed there was no way out.

But God had other plans.

Even when I was at my lowest, when I thought I had nothing left, He was working behind the scenes, preparing me for something greater than I ever imagined.

He did not just pull me out of addiction. He gave me a purpose.

Regaining My Life, Healing, Education, and Rebuilding

The year 2021 was when everything started changing.

It was not just about getting sober. It was about restoring everything I had lost. And little by little, God started putting the pieces back together.

Regaining Custody of My Child

One of the biggest miracles began in 2021 when I started the process of regaining custody of one of my children.

For years, I had believed that I would never have the chance to be a mother again. CPS had taken my children. I had spent years in addiction. I had failed them more times than I could count.

But when God restores, He does not do it halfway.

I did not just get sober. I became the mother my children deserved. I fought to prove that I had changed, that I was no longer the woman I used to be. And in 2022, I was able to bring one of my babies back home.

It was a moment I will never forget.

Holding my child in my arms again, knowing that I was finally capable of raising them, was one of the greatest gifts God ever gave me.

Healing from Hepatitis C

After years of drug use, my body had suffered greatly.

I had been diagnosed with Hepatitis C, a disease that was just another consequence of the life I had lived. I thought it would be something I had to deal with forever.

But God is a healer.

In 2021, I was completely cured of Hepatitis C. It was another sign that God was restoring not just my soul but also my body.

Pursuing a Career; Medical Billing and Coding

For so many years, I felt like I had no future. I had been homeless, in and out of jail, and surviving off of whatever I could get. The idea of having a real job, a career, something stable felt impossible.

But God made a way.

In 2021, I completed a Medical Billing and Coding certification. It was my first step toward building a future beyond addiction.

Shortly after, I got a job in the medical field.

For the first time in decades, I was earning an honest living. I was working, providing for my children, and proving to myself that I was capable of more.

It was not just about the money. It was about reclaiming my life.

Becoming a Minister and Founding a Non-Profit

If you had told me years ago that I would one day stand before people as a minister, I would have laughed in disbelief. Me. A woman who had spent decades in addiction. A woman who had lost her children, been in and out of jail and walked the darkest paths.

But God specializes in using the broken for His glory.

The calling to ministry did not come all at once. It started as a whisper in my spirit. A tug at my heart that I could not ignore. I started feeling a deep urge to share my testimony, to tell people what God had done in my life.

At first, I hesitated. Who would listen to me? How could someone with my past be a vessel for God's word?

But God reminded me of something powerful. He does not call the qualified. He qualifies for the call.

So, I stepped out in faith.

I started speaking at churches, recovery meetings, and community events, sharing my journey of addiction, loss, and redemption. Every time I spoke, I saw the hope spark in someone else's eyes.

That is when I knew. This was my calling.

In 2023, I received my Minister's Certificate, officially stepping into the role that God had been preparing me for all along.

But my purpose did not stop there.

I knew I could not just talk about change. I had to create change.

In 2024, I founded House of Reconciliation, a non-profit organization dedicated to helping others break free from addiction, rebuild their lives, and walk in God's purpose.

This organization was not just a dream. It was my way of giving back. My way of making sure no one else had to go through what I did alone.

My Mission to Help Others Overcome Addiction

For almost twenty years, addiction was my prison.

It took everything from me. My children, my dignity, my health, and nearly my life.

I know what it is like to feel hopeless, lost, and completely alone.

That is why I made a promise to God. If He brought me out, I would dedicate my life to helping others find their way out, too.

Now, my mission is simple.

To reach those who are trapped in the same cycle I was in.

To tell them. You are not too far gone. God still has a purpose for your life.

To show them that recovery is possible. Redemption is possible. A new life is possible.

Through my ministry and my non-profit, I work with.

Women who have lost everything to addiction and want to rebuild their lives.

Men and women in jail who feel forgotten and need to know that their story is not over.

Mothers fighting for their children, just like I once fought for mine.

People on the streets who have been written off by society reminding them that God still sees them.

I do not just tell them my story. I walk with them through their journey.

I pray with them, cry with them, and celebrate with them.

Because I know firsthand that sometimes, all it takes is one person to believe in you and make a difference.

The Lessons I've Learned Through Faith and Perseverance

Looking back, I see that every struggle, every loss, and every moment of pain was leading me to this purpose.

Here's what I've learned:

1. God's Grace is Bigger Than Any Past Mistake.

I once believed that I was beyond saving, that I had done too much wrong to ever be redeemed.

But God's grace is limitless. He doesn't look at where you've been, and He looks at where He's taking you.

2. Addiction is a Battle, But It Can Be Won.

Recovery isn't easy. There are days when the cravings hit, when the enemy whispers lies, and when the past tries to pull you back. But with God, victory is possible.

3. Healing Takes Time, But It's Worth It.

Rebuilding relationships, especially with my children, was not instant. There were years of pain, trust issues, and wounds that had to heal.

But step by step, God restored what was lost.

4. Your Pain Has a Purpose.

Everything I went through, losing my parents, my children, my freedom, and my niece, was not in vain.

It gave me the strength and wisdom to help others. God can use even the ugliest parts of your story for something beautiful.

5. Never Underestimate the Power of Prayer.

I tried for years to get clean on my own. It wasn't until I surrendered to God that true change happened.

Prayer isn't just something we do; it's a weapon against the enemy.

From Broken to Blessed

If you had asked me years ago where I thought my life would end up, this is not what I would have imagined.

I thought I would die of addiction.

I thought I would never see my kids again.

I thought my story was over.

But God had other plans.

Today, I stand here as a living testimony that redemption is real.

I am no longer the woman I used to be.

The drugs, the pain, the past. It no longer defines me.

I am a minister, a leader, a mother, and a woman walking on purpose.

I have been broken, but now I am blessed.

I have been lost, but now I am found.

And my mission is simple.

I want to spend the rest of my life helping others find the freedom that God gave me.

This is not the end of my story.

This is just the beginning.

Chapter 8

Reflections and Final Thoughts

"And we know that in all things God works for the good of those who love Him, who have been called according to His purpose."
~Romans 8:28

Looking back on my life, I see how every struggle, every loss, and every moment of pain led me to where I am today. I once believed my story was nothing but hardship, but now I know it was preparing me for something greater. My past does not define me. It has shaped me, but it is not who I am.

What I Would Tell My Younger Self

If I could go back and speak to my younger self, I would tell her that she is stronger than she knows. I would tell her that she does not have to search for love in people who do not value her. I would tell her that her mistakes do not make her unworthy of happiness. I would tell her that no matter how dark things seem, there is always hope.

I would remind her that she does not have to carry the weight of her pain alone. I would tell her to hold on a little longer because her story is not over. I would tell her that God has a plan for her life, even if she cannot see it yet.

Encouragement for Others Struggling with Addiction

To anyone struggling with addiction, I want you to know that it is never too late to change. No matter how many times you have failed, no matter how far gone you think you are, there is always a way forward. Recovery is possible. Healing is possible.

You do not have to do it alone. There are people who will stand by you and help you through it. Ask for help. Take it one day at a time. Do not let shame keep you from seeking the support you need.

Your past does not have to determine your future. If you are willing to fight for a better life, it is within reach. The road to recovery is not easy, but it is worth it.

The Power of Faith and Surrender

I tried for years to fix my life on my own. I thought I could control my addiction, but I kept falling back into the same patterns. It was not until I surrendered to God that real change happened.

Faith gave me the strength to keep going when I wanted to give up. It reminded me that I was never alone, even in my darkest moments. Letting go and trusting God was the hardest thing I had to do, but it was also the best decision I ever made.

God restored what I lost. He gave me a new life and a new purpose. If He can do it for me, He can do it for anyone.

Your Story is Not Over

This book is not just my story. It is proof that no one is beyond redemption. No matter where you are in life, this is not the end. A new beginning is possible. You are not too broken to be healed. You are not too lost to be found.

Take the first step. Keep moving forward. Believe that a better life is waiting for you.

Chapter 9

My Life in Timeline

Life is a journey filled with moments that shape us, break us, and rebuild us. Looking back, I see how every event, both good and bad, led me to where I am today. This is my story in its rawest form: a journey of survival, loss, addiction, and, ultimately, redemption.

2003: The Beginning of Struggles

At just 14 years old, I became a mother. In January 2003, I gave birth to my first child, a responsibility I was nowhere near ready for. I was still a child myself, trying to figure out life, and now I had a baby depending on me.

That same year, in November, my world shattered. My mother passed away, leaving a void in my life that nothing could fill. The pain was unbearable, and I had no idea how to cope. That night, at her funeral, I tried meth for the first time. It was supposed to numb the pain, but instead, it opened the door to a new kind of suffering.

By December 2003, I had started using heroin and cocaine. The drugs became an escape, a way to silence the grief that consumed me. The day after my first experience with heroin, I dropped out of school. My education no longer mattered. My future no longer mattered. All I cared about was finding my next high.

2004: Losing My Father

In January 2004, just two months after losing my mother, my father was hospitalized. He went into a coma, and suddenly, I was facing the possibility of losing the only parent I had left.

That same month, I earned my GED, a small achievement in the midst of chaos. But there was no time to celebrate. I was watching my father slip away.

In July 2004, my worst fear became reality. My father passed away, leaving me completely alone.

I spent the rest of 2004 living with my sister, trying to find some stability, but the weight of addiction was already too strong.

2005-2006: Falling Deeper

By 2005, I moved into my own place, but my addiction followed me. I continued using heroin, convinced that I could not function without it.

That year, my daughter's leg was broken. I will never forget the fear I felt when I took her to the hospital, knowing that CPS would get involved. And they did. In 2005, CPS took my daughter away from me. I was devastated, but instead of fighting for her, I fell deeper into addiction.

By 2006, I was no longer just snorting heroin. I had started shooting up. The one thing I swore I would never do became my new reality.

That same year, I found out I was pregnant again, but my relationship with my child's father had already fallen apart. While I was still carrying his child, we separated.

When I gave birth to my second child in 2006, CPS took him too. Another piece of me was gone.

2007: A New Addiction

As if heroin was not enough, in 2007, I was introduced to crack cocaine. I thought I had already hit rock bottom, but crack cocaine took me to places I never imagined. It controlled me in a way I never expected. I was no longer just surviving; and I was completely enslaved to addiction.

2017: A Mother's Worst Nightmare

In 2017, I experienced one of the deepest pains a mother can endure. I gave birth to a stillborn baby. The grief was unbearable. I had already lost so much in my life, but this loss was different. This was a child who never even had the chance to live.

2020: A Second Chance

By 2020, my body had been through more than I ever thought possible. That year, I suffered a placenta abruption while pregnant. I flatlined three times. Doctors fought to bring me back, but after everything I had been through, even death itself could not take me.

After I survived, I found myself under investigation for my child's death. It was yet another blow in a life already filled with hardship.

But something shifted in 2020. It was the year I finally decided to start getting clean.

2021: The Year of Restoration

January 1, 2021, was the day that changed everything. My niece, who was like a sister to me, died from a fentanyl overdose. Her death shook me to my core. I knew I could not keep living this way.

Later that year, I left a toxic relationship that had been holding me back for far too long. I started fighting for my life, for my children, and for my future.

For the first time in years, I saw progress.

In 2022, I regained custody of one of my children. After starting the process in 2021 and spending years watching them grow up from a distance, I finally had the chance to be a mother again.

That same year, I was cured of Hepatitis C, a disease that had been a result of my years of drug use.

I also took a step toward building a stable future. I earned a Medical Billing and Coding certification and got a job in the medical field. After years of surviving on the streets, I finally had honest work.

2023: A New Calling

In 2023, I officially became a minister. After everything I had been through, I knew that my story had a greater purpose. I wanted to help others find the same redemption I had found. I wanted to use my testimony to bring hope to those who felt lost.

2024: Giving Back

In 2024, I founded House of Reconciliation, a non-profit dedicated to helping people overcome addiction and rebuild their lives. It was the fulfillment of a promise I made to God that if He saved me, I would spend the rest of my life helping others find their way out, too.

A Life Transformed

My journey has been filled with pain, but it has also been filled with redemption. I have lost, but I have also gained. I have been broken, but I have been made whole again.

Every moment, every struggle, every loss has led me here.

This is my story. This is my testimony. This is proof that no matter how far you have fallen, there is always a way back.

Chapter 10

Turning Pain into Power

"They triumphed over him by the blood of the Lamb and by the word of their testimony."
~Revelation 12:11

For years, my story was one of survival. I lived through addiction, loss, and pain that I would not wish on anyone. Today, my story is more than just survival. It is about empowerment.

I once believed that my past would always define me and that the choices I had made would forever dictate my future. Now, I know that our struggles do not have to keep us in bondage. Instead, they can be the foundation of something greater.

Pain, when given to God, can be turned into purpose. Every trial, every setback, and every battle can be used to uplift and empower others. My story is not just my own. It is a message to anyone who feels trapped, lost, or unworthy of a second chance.

The Power of Owning Your Story

For a long time, I carried shame and guilt for the life I had lived. I wanted to hide my past, to pretend that the years of addiction and brokenness never happened. The truth is hiding your story gives power to the pain.

It was not until I started sharing my testimony that I realized the true power of my journey. When I spoke openly about my struggles, people began to listen. They saw hope in my words because if God could transform my life, He could do the same for them.

Owning my story allowed me to take back control. I was no longer the victim of my past. I was victorious over it.

Using My Journey to Inspire Others

Through my experiences, I have had the opportunity to

- Encourage women who have lost custody of their children to fight for their recovery and rebuild their relationships.
- Help those in addiction understand that sobriety is possible and that they are not beyond redemption.

- Speak to incarcerated individuals who feel hopeless, reminding them that their past does not have to define their future.
- Mentor young people who are walking the same dangerous path I once did, showing them the consequences of addiction and the beauty of a changed life.

Each time I share my testimony, someone is impacted. Someone sees themselves in my words. Someone realizes that if I could break free, so can they.

Empowerment Through Faith and Action

True empowerment does not just come from sharing our stories. It comes from living in the transformation that God has given us. It means:

- Taking responsibility for our growth and choosing to live differently.
- Helping others by offering support, mentorship, and encouragement.
- Building something greater than ourselves, like I did with the House of Reconciliation.
- Trusting that our past does not disqualify us. It prepares us to serve.

The most powerful thing we can do is use what we have been through to make a difference. That is how pain turns into power. That is how we break generational cycles. That is how we empower others to rise above their circumstances.

Your Story Can Change Lives

I am living proof that no matter how dark your past is, it can be used for something greater.

If you are struggling, if you feel like your story is too messy, too broken, or too painful to be of any value, I want you to know that you have a purpose.

Your pain can be turned into power. Your testimony can bring healing to someone else. Your life still has meaning.

Do not be afraid to own your story. Do not be afraid to let your past become someone else's source of hope.

This is how we rise.

This is how we empower.

This is how we turn our trials into triumphs.

Acknowledgments

First and foremost, I want to thank God for His mercy, grace, and unwavering love. Without Him, I would not be here today. He carried me through my darkest moments and gave me the strength to keep going when I had nothing left. This book is a testament to His power to restore, redeem, and transform even the most broken lives.

To my children, thank you for loving me despite my past. I know I was not always the mother you deserved, but I have spent every day fighting to be better for you. You are my greatest blessing, and I am so proud to be your mother.

To my family, especially my sister and aunt, thank you for standing in the gap when I couldn't. Thank you for taking care of my children when I wasn't able to. Your love and support gave them the stability they needed, and for that, I will always be grateful.

To the friends, mentors, and church family who prayed for me, encouraged me, and refused to give up on me, I thank you. Your belief in my ability to change helped push me toward a better life.

To the House of Reconciliation and all those who have supported my mission, thank you for walking alongside me on this journey. What we are building together is bigger than any one of us, and I am honored to be part of a movement that brings hope and healing to others.

Finally, to anyone reading this book who is struggling, know that you are not alone. Your story is not over. I pray that my journey gives you hope, that my mistakes teach you lessons, and that my testimony reminds you that God is still in the business of changing lives.

With love and gratitude,

Christina.